C000186222

Stories of World War I

Faith in Action

Edited by
Raymond Edwards

Compiled by Sr Fabiola Fernandes

*All booklets are published thanks to the
generous support of the members of the
Catholic Truth Society*

CATHOLIC TRUTH SOCIETY

PUBLISHERS TO THE HOLY SEE

Contents

All rights reserved. First published 2014 by The Incorporated Catholic Truth Society, 40-46 Harleyford Road London SE11 5AY Tel: 020 7640 0042 Fax: 020 7640 0046. © 2014 The Incorporated Catholic Truth Society.

Inside images: Page 9 © Hulton-Deutsch Collection/CORBIS; Page 29 © E. W. Weigle/National Geographic Society/Corbis; Page 53 © Bettmann/CORBIS.

ISBN 978 1 86082 905 5

Introduction

It is now a hundred years since the outbreak of the First World War, the Great War, the war that broke the centuries-old shape of Europe and, after five years of carnage and destruction, arguably inaugurated for much of Europe a further seventy years of misery that only lifted, in part, with the collapse of communism in the closing years of the twentieth century. It goes almost without saying, too, that the Second World War is in one sense only an interrupted continuation of the First, and without it is hardly conceivable.

That, at any rate, is how the War may appear to us now; but we can learn much, not only historical details but of human sympathy, by looking at what people at the time said and wrote about their experience. We are lazily accustomed to picture the Great War as an experience of overmastering futility, a foul amalgam of mud and despair; but we should be suspicious, perhaps, of imposing on raw experience a template drawn too exclusively from the opinions of a small sample of literary men. The 1920s and 1930s were keen to emphasise the futility of all war, and found the English "war poets", and a series of disillusioned memoirs (by Graves, Sassoon, and others) a potent tool in doing so. This view, spiced with a frankly libellous and grossly unfair image of supposedly callous and incompetent generals, has largely conditioned how the War has been seen since.

But this was not the approach taken by most who wrote at the time, both soldiers and civilians. They were, in great part, convinced that the war was a necessary struggle against a brutal tyranny - German militarism - and was a cause which ennobled the sacrifices it demanded. They did not ignore or minimise the horrors of war; but they would not concede that they were pointless. The vast majority of contemporary evidence, including that from soldiers at the front, is of this sort: appalled at the effects of war, but convinced it was done for a righteous cause. This sort of attitude is today out of fashion, in Britain at any rate; but we should not ignore or dismiss a thing because we find it strange. Christian theology has generally allowed that a "just war" may exist, and that fighting in one may be both virtuous and, even, of obligation. Our forefathers a century ago were largely convinced that their war against Germany was such a just war; we should do them the courtesy of at least allowing they might have been right to think so.

From the very outbreak of the War, the Catholic Truth Society (CTS) was involved with the British war effort. Most importantly, it co-operated with the War Office in providing very large numbers of Simple Prayer Books for Catholic soldiers and sailors, and also other devotional material. Several booklets were also published during the War describing how it specifically affected Catholics; and it is some of this material that is here reprinted.

The first part of this booklet has been compiled from two CTS pamphlets first published in 1915 - *Some Stories of the War* and *More Stories of the War*. Most of the anecdotes, then, are from the War's early stages, when Britain's armies were made up of pre-War regular soldiers, reservists, and members of the Territorial Army. The first wartime volunteers, Kitchener's Armies, did not for the most part see action until 1916, on the Somme, so we hear little from them here.

A good number of the stories concern French or Belgian Catholics, both clergy and laity; not a few relate stories of German atrocities that, until comparatively recently, it was usual to dismiss or minimise as wartime propaganda, but which more recent research has tended to bear out. There was indeed a deliberate policy of terror on the part of the German troops in Belgium and occupied France, both on an individual *ad hoc* level and on a larger scale - such as, most famously, the deliberate destruction of the ancient university town of Leuven (Louvain) and the burning of the University Library there. The German army was afraid of organised resistance amongst Belgian civilians, and thousands, including woman and children, were killed and more brutalised in an attempt to discourage this. Before the War, Belgium had a deserved reputation as the most devoutly Catholic nation in Europe (see, for instance, Ronald Knox's autobiographical *Spiritual Aeneid*);[1] its clergy and religious were numerous and highly visible, and formed an obvious target for an invader's acts of exemplary punishment. This deliberate and savage assault on the populace of a neutral country (allied propaganda regularly talked of "The Rape of Belgium" or its "martyrdom") was at the heart of a case for the conflict as a just war. Not all Germans were reckoned to be monsters, though; several of the stories here recognise them as fellow-Christians, acting according to their lights.

The religious character of the French and British armies was not obviously Catholic. France had, before the War, gone through another of its periodic bouts of anti-clericalism; religious orders had been expelled from the country, schools taken away from them, and church property confiscated. The French government in 1914 declined to exempt clergy from military service, and so thousands of priests fought in the trenches as ordinary soldiers. Many of the stories collected here concern them; they illustrate, amongst other things, how the War effected a partial reconciliation between Church and State, moved by the simple bravery of many priests in uniform. Religion traditionally flourishes during wartime; immanent death, daily and unavoidable, tends to give the last things an immediacy, and the consolations of religion a force, that in peacetime they often lack. Various stories illustrate the piety of French soldiers at the front; we should not forget, perhaps, that it was the enthusiasm of *poilus* in the trenches that first made devotion to St Thérèse of Lisieux widespread.

For many, perhaps most of the British soldiers, wartime in Belgium and France would represent their first experience of a living Catholic culture, rather than the childhood bogeys of popery they would have been familiar with. Most were impressed by what they saw. We see here, also, how struck many soldiers were by the Catholic custom of prayer for the dead, something traditionally dismissed in Anglican apologetics as archetypal popish superstition. The losses of the War, which touched directly almost every family in the country, played a great part in dismantling this particular element of anti-Catholic prejudice. Remembrance Day may now seem unexceptionable, but its universal observance in Britain from 1919 on represents, in terms of public religion, little short of a revolution.

The second part is taken from a pamphlet of January 1917, *The Catholic Chaplains in the Great War*. As the writer points out, although Catholics had served in the British Army since the late eighteenth century, there had been no official provision for military chaplains to minister to them until the Crimean War in the 1850s. The Great War saw an enormous expansion of Catholic chaplaincy in both Army and Navy, strongly encouraged by Cardinal

Bourne and the great majority of the hierarchy. The Army's Catholic chaplains, whose instinct was to be close to their men so as to be on hand to give the Last Rites, quickly gained a general reputation for courage under fire. Their role was not always exclusively spiritual. During the First Battle of Ypres, so the story goes, at a critical moment all the officers of the 2nd Munster Fusiliers were killed or wounded, and their chaplain, Fr Francis Gleeson, took down his chaplain's badges and assumed command of the battalion until it was relieved. The stories collected below are eloquent of this type of heroic faith.

The *Chaplains* pamphlet was put together by Andrew Hilliard Atteridge, a journalist and popular historian; he may also have helped with compiling the two other texts drawn on here, although they mainly compiled by Eileen Boland, wife to John Boland, the Olympic tennis gold medallist, at that time MP for South Kerry, later CTS General Secretary.

In all cases the original text has been given unchanged, although some passages have been omitted for reasons of space, and the order of some of the material has been altered for emphasis; editorial additions are given in italics.

British troops arrive in France, 1914.

Stories of the War

It is some consolation that war, with all its horrors, is lightened by the instances of devotion and sacrifice which always emerge from an otherwise tragic and terrible record. The war now being waged has already supplied an abundance of such material. Out of this abundance the following pages have been compiled; they relate some of the many stories which throw into vivid light the power of Faith to serve the cause of Fatherland.

Priests in action

"Eighty-seven Catholic priests and one hundred and twenty-seven nuns have been awarded the Legion of Honour by the French Government for the services rendered to troops in the field of action." So says the *Times* (4th December) within four months of the outbreak of the war of 1914. We have not all the details of the heroic acts which earned this distinction, but enough has been published to show that the priests have followed, in the letter and in the spirit, the instructions of the Bishop of Poitiers: "Before all and above all be a priest; that is, a man of duty among your heroic brothers in arms. By word and example raise their hearts to God. The reputation and honour of the clergy of France

British soldiers cross barren ground during WWI ca. 1914-1918.

reorganisation of the Army carried out after the war, Catholic chaplains became a permanent part of the establishment; and, though their numbers were limited, before long one was to be found at every important military centre, and it became a recognised practice to attach at least one Catholic chaplain to every expeditionary force employed in our minor frontier wars. Catholic chaplains belonging to the Regular Army establishment received the same pay and relative rank as the Anglican and Presbyterian chaplains - joining as chaplains of the fourth class (ranking with captains), and rising by length of service to the grade of chaplains of the first class, with the relative rank of Colonel. In the case of military operations on a large scale (such as those of the South African War), additional temporary chaplains were appointed.

With the enormous increase of the numbers of the Army which has taken place during the present war, the Catholic chaplains already attached to the regular establishment were far too few in numbers, and at the very outset the War Office asked our bishops to provide an additional number of priests, who would be temporarily commissioned as chaplains. There were some complaints in the first months of the war that the numbers thus provided were inadequate; but it may safely be said that this was not the result of any negligence or ill-will on the part of the War Office authorities, but rather of the general failure to recognise at the beginning of operations the vast scale on which they were to be conducted. In its dealings with the religious interests of our Catholic soldiers in the

the Naval Division at the Dardanelles, gave the Catholics the badge of the Sacred Heart to wear when going into action. He was then asked by hundreds of non-Catholics to give it to them, and in several of the battalions all the men went into battle wearing this Catholic badge on their helmets.

Some letters published in a Preston newspaper from soldiers of the Lancashire Regiment give us striking pictures of the influence of the Catholic chaplain in times of danger and stress. Thus, a non-Catholic soldier writing to his parents tells of what occurred on the voyage of the transport through the Mediterranean and after the landing in Gallipoli:

"You know I am not allowed to say much, but I will tell you how we landed. We had a very rough voyage, chased by German submarines. Well, a Catholic Father sailed with us, and a good job too. We thought we were done for, but he was like a good shepherd. I learned how to pray then if I never prayed before. I think if I am spared I shall take care to lead a good Christian life. I shall never forget the way he taught us to pray. It is surprising how the men ran after him shouting, 'Bless me, sir, same as you have done that man.' Well, he blessed us all on ship and everybody kissed a cross he had. It seemed strange to me, but I did what they did. It is surprising how the men run after him, and the men do pray on the field. We all wish he could stop with us but he cannot be with us always. There are several fathers and ministers,

but none take same as him. I don't know his name,
but J.'s mother will know his name, as they say he is
from Preston. I will never forget his kindness. If I am
spared I think I shall follow his fold."

The heroic death of Father Finn at the landing in the
Dardanelles has already been described. The wonder is
that there were not more casualties among the chaplains
attached to the expedition. On the Western Front there
were times when officers and men had a rest outside the
fire zone, but in the Gallipoli peninsula there was not a
square yard of ground which was not from time to time
under fire. To find a place where an altar could be set up
and Mass be said, with some prospect of safety for the
chaplain and his soldier congregation, was no easy matter,
and there were some very narrow escapes. Thus, one
morning, when the chaplain of the Naval Division was
saying Mass for his men, at a spot which was supposed to
be comparatively safe, a Turkish battery on the Asiatic side
began to throw long range shells across the Straits, and
twice during the Mass a shell struck a tree not far from the
altar; but, happily, in both cases it failed to burst.

Father William Leighton, of Fanworth, in Lancashire,
was with the 9th Warwickshires in the Suvla Bay landing
in August 1915, and was mentioned in dispatches and
received the Military Cross for his gallantry in the
unsuccessful attack on the Chunuk Bair. The Warwicks

went into action a thousand strong, but after the day's fighting only one hundred and thirty men were left, and of the officers the Catholic chaplain was the only one who was neither killed nor wounded. During the advance against the ridge he was close up to the firing-line, and saved the lives of many of the wounded by giving them first aid and placing them under cover. A soldier's letter, describing the fighting at the point where the force from Suvla Bay came in touch with the advance from Anzac, tells how during the whole of the day another of the chaplains, Father John Linehan, was moving about between the firing-line and the dressing-station, bringing in wounded men on his shoulders - Australians, New Zealanders, and Ghurkas.

Recognised for their service

More than twenty Catholic chaplains have already been mentioned in dispatches and granted various military decorations. One of the "mentions in dispatches" is that of Father McMullen, the chaplain to General Townshend's force at Kut-el-Amara, who is now a prisoner of the Turks in Asia Minor.

Only when the war is over will it be possible to attempt to make anything like an adequate record of the work done by the Catholic chaplains in the armies and navies of the belligerent Powers. What has been here written is only a slight sketch of what they have been doing with our own fighting men. It would have been easy to give many more extracts from soldiers' letters, but the few that have been quoted are a fair representation of the general character of them all. From all the Fronts there come again and again the same testimonies to the unsparing efforts of the chaplains to be of service to their men, both in body and soul, the same stories of perils cheerfully encountered and hardships endured without a murmur, and at the same time abundant evidence that the influence of the chaplain extends far beyond his Catholic flock, that non-Catholics recognise his devotion to his sacred ministry and come to him voluntarily, for spiritual help, their request often including their asking him to instruct them and receive them into the Catholic Church.

Endnotes

[1] "the extraordinary devotion of the people wherever we went, and especially at Bruges, struck home with an immeasurable contrast to the churches of one's own country, half-filled on Sunday, shadowily peopled on weekdays by a faithful few. Bruges itself we declared to be the Holy City ..." *A Spiritual Aeneid* (London, Longmans, Green & Co., 1918) p.84. *Knox first visited Belgium in 1910, when he was preparing for ordination into the Church of England.*

[2] *Émile Combes was French Prime Minister between 1902 and 1905; his ministry implemented the laws that led to the end of religious schools and the flight of religious orders into exile. Aristide Briand, architect of the anti-clerical laws, was Prime Minister several times, notably between 1909 and 1911, again in 1913, and from 1915 to 1917. He was later Prime Minister again for three periods in the 1920s.*

[3] *Pierre Corneille was a French playwright of the seventeenth century; the war of 1870 is the Franco-Prussian War, in which the German victory was still bitterly resented by the French.*

[4] *"Monkey" here is probably soldier's slang for potted meat.*

[5] *This uniform detail dates the story to the early days of the War; the French soldier's characteristic red trousers were soon replaced by ones of a colour less calculated to draw fire.*

[6] *Uhlans were lance-armed cavalry in the German or Austrian service; ulan is originally a Turkic word for "warrior", adopted first to describe Polish light cavalry in the eighteenth century, and later extended to soldiers of other nationalities similarly armed. By 1914, all German cavalry carried lances, whether or not they belonged to the historic Uhlan regiments, so the word is often used as a loose equivalent for "German cavalryman".*

[7] *The 75, or soixante-quinze, was a French field gun of particular efficiency.*

[8] *A "marmite" is a type of French cooking-pot (which features on the label of the proprietary yeast extract), and is here used by transference to refer to a type of German heavy mortar shell of similar shape.*

[9] *Two further Stonyhurst old boys were awarded the V.C. in the Great War.*

[10] *The Military Service Act of March 1916 introduced conscription; until then recruitment to the armed services was wholly voluntary.*

[11] *Anzac refers to the Australian and New Zealand Army Corps, who first saw action in Gallipoli.*

[12] *Sir Garnet Wolseley, later Field Marshal Viscount Wolseley, was a massively distinguished and proverbially successful British general of the Victorian age.*

[13] *Eighty-five lives were lost of the two hundred and twenty-nine aboard the ship when it ran aground in a storm on 30th October 1914.*

[14] *The bulk of the pre-War Regular Army formed the original British Expeditionary Force (BEF) of 1914, the renowned "Old Contemptibles"; the great majority of that Army were casualties of the first few months' fighting in France, culminating in the First Battle of Ypres, where it fought the German Army to a standstill at the cost of most of its remaining men. Thereafter almost all of Britain's forces were made up of Territorial reservists or wartime volunteers ("Kitchener's Armies").*

[15] John Masefield, *Gallipoli*, p. 42.

[16] *He saved two young sailors from burning to death in a fire in a gun turret. Such fires caused catastrophic explosions and the subsequent loss of a number of British ships at Jutland.*

[17] *Field Marshal Sir John French, created Viscount French in 1916 and later Earl of Ypres, commanded the BEF from the start of the War until 1915; he was replaced by Sir Douglas Haig.*

A world of Catholic reading at your fingertips...

Catholic Faith, Life & Truth for all

www.CTSbooks.org

twitter: @CTSpublishers

facebook.com/CTSpublishers

Catholic Truth Society, Publishers to the Holy See.